W9-DBO-184

Start Right Reader

GRADE 1 · BOOK 6

Printed in the U.S.A.

ISBN 978-1-328-82593-3

13 0877 26 25 24 23

4500863693 B C D E F G

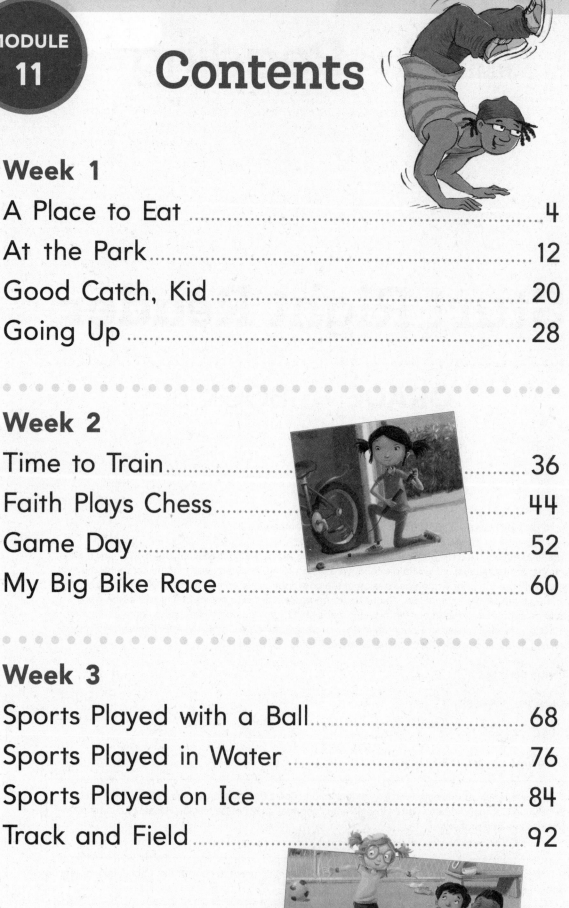

Contents

MODULE 12

Week 1

Week 2

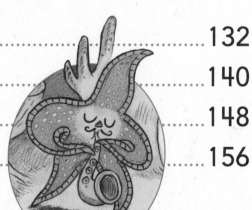

Week 3

Get Started

Meet Grace and her mom and dad. They are visiting a big town.

Where will Grace, Mom, and Dad go? What will they see and do in the big town? Read to find out!

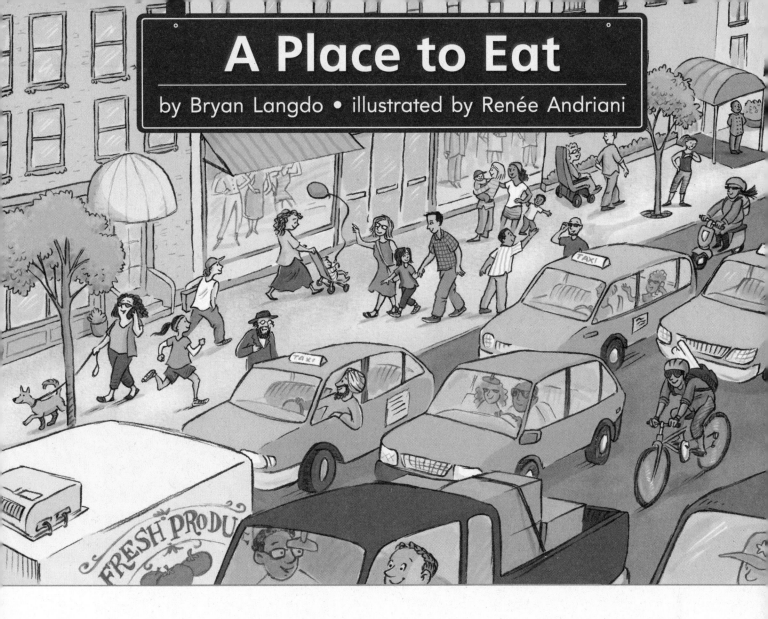

A Place to Eat

by Bryan Langdo • illustrated by Renée Andriani

My name is Grace. I'm in a big town with my mom and dad. We walk through huge crowds. There is so much to see! Wow!

Buses, trucks, and cars zoom by so fast. Many of these cars are yellow. The yellow cars are cabs. Beep-beep! People are in such a hurry in this place! It sings with loud sounds, and to me, it is just perfect!

We walk past an art store that sells paintings and art objects. The next store we pass is a bookstore with books and old maps.

I peek in a store window and see a pretty blue gown hanging next to blouses on racks. We go into this store to see if Mom will get a new scarf.

"Grace, look out," Mom says in a loud voice as I start to step down from the curb.

I see the sign that looks like a red hand. It means **Don't Walk**. I stop right there.

We watch cars drive past us. I can't count them or all the people on bikes.

"Now we can go," Dad tells us. We look right and left before we step off the curb.

Mom, Dad, and I needed to eat and sit for a while, but where would we go?

Dad had an answer! "I can use a map on my cell," he said, tilting it so that Mom and I could see. "It will help us find a good place to eat and show us how to get there." In no time, Dad had found a place for us to eat and had a map that led right to it.

"Let's go!" Dad said, leading the way. We make a right. Here, we make a left.

"Watch out, Dad!" I said as he started to trip on a curb. His cell fell. Crack!

Dad looked down and frowned. His cell wasn't working.

"Well, that's that," said Dad. "Now how will we find a good place to eat?"

I sniff the air. I smell something good!

"I know where we can go," I told Mom and Dad. "It can't be too far! Let's follow our noses."

My nose led us to the right place. I pointed out the shop to Mom and Dad.

"Here we are!" I said. "I hope the food is as good to eat as it is to smell!"

Story Word Clues

Read each clue. Find the correct word in the story.

1. I have the letters **ou**. I hang on racks in a store. What word am I?

2. I have the letters **ow**. Dad did this when his phone cracked. What word am I?

Check your work with a partner. Take turns making up clues about other story words for your partner to solve.

Blend and Read

1. cow   crown   wow   brown   now

2. sound   mouth   foul   mouse   south

3. ferns   curb   boots   book   burn

4. fowl   vow   spout   howl   slouch

5. There are many loud sounds in town.

6. Where is the store that sells blouses?

At the Park

by Bryan Langdo
illustrated by Renée Andriani

Soon Mom, Dad, and I were walking down long flights of steps deep into the ground. That's where the subway trains run. We will take a train to a park.

We had to wait for the train. I watched a few people smile and sing songs while we waited. People started to clap and drop money for them into a hat.

I heard a train before I saw it rolling up the tracks. It sounded much louder than the cars and trucks above us as it sped at us with brakes howling and came to a stop.

Mom looked at the train and let us know it wasn't the right train for us. When the right train came, Mom and Dad held my hands. We had to stick together in the crowd.

Our train zoomed through dark tunnels. Lights flashed past my window. I counted the stops. Then it was our stop, and Mom said, "This is where we get off. Let's go!"

We walked up steep flights of steps and came to a part of town that looked new to us. We went into a lush, green park.

We could see a big crowd and hear a booming voice saying that a show would be starting soon. Wow! This place is not like my hometown at all.

A man pressed a button and sounds rocked the park. His songs had such a good sound that Mom and I started to clap and tap our feet. Dad started to dance.

Then the man started to dance. His feet slid into dance steps with ease. He looked like he could be on slick ice, the way he seemed to glide and still not miss a beat.

Then he did flips and walked on his hands. He was bending, jumping, and turning to the beat like a rubber band!

"Wow!" I sighed. "How did he do that?"

After that, a girl got down on the ground and started to spin fast, like a top. Then she started to spin just as fast on her head, maybe faster! It looked like she could keep going and never stop.

Mom, Dad, and I had fun watching this show—for free! It was such a blast doing new things on this trip into town.

Rhyming Story Words

1. Look in the story for words that rhyme with **round**. Write each word you find.

2. Look in the story for words that rhyme with **brown**. Write each word you find.

3. Look at your list of words. Circle the word that tells what you see when you look down.

Poetry Break

Read the poem with a partner.

A Trip to Town

We **walk** around the town.
We **point** to the left and **right**.
We **walk** uptown and down
Where we can see the sights.

A **voice** says, "**Watch** this flip!"
We **answer** with a grin.
I'll **write** about my trip
When I am home again.

Good Catch, Kid

by Bryan Langdo • illustrated by Renée Andriani

"Where will we go next?" I asked Mom and Dad. "Will we go to a store? Will we go to see a play?" I asked many things, but Mom and Dad didn't answer me!

"You'll see," Mom told me with a little grin. Dad's smile was wide, but he didn't tell me where we would be going next.

We went down a long road and made a few more turns. Dad stood still and pointed to a big gate down the road.

"We are going there!" he told us.

Yay! We were going to watch a game!

We joined a line and went inside. Dad paid for us. He gave me my ticket stub. I will keep it with me always!

"Let's get snacks on the way to our seats," Mom said. We got food and drinks at a stand. I asked for a hot dog. It smelled so good! I couldn't wait to eat it!

We found our seats and sat down at last. I peeled the foil off my hot dog. It was very hot, so I waited a bit. Then I took my first bite. Yum!

A batboy handed a bat to a man. The man walked up to home plate. His shirt had a big blue ten on it.

A loud voice spoke to the crowd. "Now at bat is Roy Cowboy Clark!" There's the pitch! Roy swung hard, but he missed.

"You can do it, Roy!" a boy yelled out.

Roy swung again. This time it was a hit!
It came right at us. Then it hit a railing.
I jumped and reached up as far as I could,
and it landed right in my hands!

"That looked like it was going to fly out
of the park!" Dad yelled.

The game ended too soon! We followed the crowd and left the stands.

On our way out, I heard a voice saying, "Good catch, kid!" It was Roy Cowboy Clark, and he had a pen in his hand!

"Nice hit, Roy Clark," I answered. He asked for my prize. I watched him write his name and **Good Catch** on it. Wow!

Setting

A story's setting is **where** and **when** it takes place. Think about the stories. Then answer the questions.

1. How does the setting change in each story? How is it the same?

2. What else might happen in a setting like the big town in the stories?

Talk about your answers with a group.

Blend and Read

1. frown   coin   clown   join   pout

2. boil   found   proud   spoil   point

3. crane   breath   teach   tread   wait

4. snout   choice   moist   grouch   toil

5. Grace points to a spot to sit down.

6. Roy Cowboy Clark likes to bat.

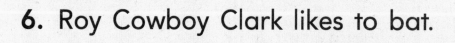

Going Up

by Bryan Langdo • illustrated by Renée Andriani

Now it is late in the day. Mom and Dad tell me we have one more place to go before we start to head for home.

"Where will we go?" I ask them.

"We're going up," Dad tells me. He looks up and points. I crane my neck to see where Dad is pointing.

"We're going to the very top," Mom says.

We step in, and Dad presses the top button. The doors start to shut when we hear a voice say, "Hold the doors, please!"

Dad holds them, and a man gets in with us. He smiles and nods to Dad. Then more people fit in. At last the doors glide shut, and we are on our way up.

We zoom up to the top.

"Let's step outside," says Mom. "Hang on to your hat. The breeze whips by up here with a lot of force."

Mom is right! It feels as if the breeze whisks my words right out of my mouth! We are up so high! When I look down, the people look like ants, and the cars look like little toy cars.

Mom hands me a coin, and I drop it into a slot. I peer through two holes for my eyes. I can see even more now because I can see so very far.

I see birds resting on a ledge and a girl planting seeds in a rooftop garden. Cats nap on a bench near her. There is so much to see!

The sun is starting to set. Lights start to blink on in windows. Boy, is this fun!

Mom looks at her watch and says, "I think it's time for us to go home."

"Yes, let's call it a day," says Dad.

I think about Roy Clark and the game. I think about the park. I ask if we can make one last stop.

"Where do you want to stop?" asks Dad. "A toy shop?"

"No," I answer him. "I want to go to a bookstore so I can get a new notebook. I want to write a story about things we did today. I don't want to forget a thing."

Then I added, "Thanks so much, both of you. This was just the best trip to town!"

Turn and Talk

Reread the four stories. Then answer
these questions.

1. What are some things that Grace does
   on her trip to town?

2. Why does Grace want a notebook?

3. Which part of the trip would **you** like to
   take with Grace? Why?

Turn and talk about your answers with
a partner.

Get Started

Do you play a game or sport? You will be reading about kids who play many different games and sports.

How do the kids get good at the games and sports they play? Do they win? Do they lose? Read to find out!

Time to Train

by Jia Lee

illustrated by Peter Francis

Each weekend is the same for Shawn. He gets up at dawn and jumps out of bed. He dashes down the hall to eat with his dad. His dad serves him food like eggs, toast with jam or peanut butter, and milk.

"Thanks, Dad. That was good," Shawn always says when he is done. He dresses, and he grabs his bag and water bottle.

"It's time to train!" Shawn says as he and his dad hop in the car and drive into town. When he gets there, Shawn knows where to go. He sees many people he knows there. They are all training.

One woman works out with a ball. Other people warm up before they work out.

Shawn warms up, too. He bends and twists and reaches up high.

"All set?" his coach asks. "Let's start with the high bar."

Shawn puts chalk on his hands. He claps his hands and rubs them together. Chalk helps him get a good grip on the bar so he will not slip and fall off it.

Shawn jumps up and grabs the high bar. He swings his feet. He bends at the waist. He swings higher and higher, and then all the way around the bar. He flips and grabs the bar. He makes big swings and then lets go, twists, and lands on his feet.

"Nice job!" his coach calls to him.

"Thanks, Coach!" Shawn says.

Shawn is done on the high bar for now, so he walks over to the rings. The rings hang on long straps.

Shawn grips the rings. He pulls himself up and lifts his legs, keeping them together. He is trying to bend only at the waist. He turns upside down, holding his arms taut. It is hard to hold still like this.

The vault is the last thing Shawn will work on today. He takes long strides as he runs up to what is called a horse. He launches himself in a solid jump. His hands slap the horse. He pushes off, and he is in the air! He flips, twirls, and lands on his feet.

"Well done, Shawn," says Coach. "That was a good vault! You worked hard today!"

Rhyming Word Hunt

Find the word in the story that fits each set of clues. Write the word.

1. This word rhymes with **lawn**.
   It tells when Shawn gets up.

2. This word rhymes with **talk**.
   Shawn puts it on his hands.

3. This word rhymes with **faults**.
   Shawn does this last.

Blend and Read

1. yawn   small   chalk   walk   wall

2. claw   fault   crawl   taut   hawk

3. town   crowd   ground   shout   sound

4. sidewalk   sawdust   cornstalk   already

5. On weekends, Shawn gets up at dawn.

6. Shawn did well on the vault.

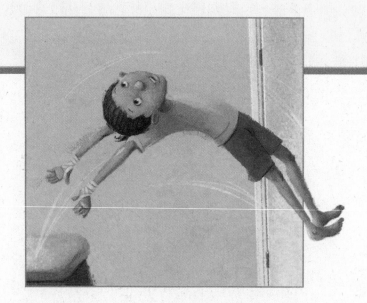

Faith Plays Chess

by Jia Lee

illustrated by Peter Francis

Faith bit her lip. She felt small walking into the big hall. The place was full of kids, but no one was talking.

Faith was here to play chess. She was good at the game. She knew that each kid in this hall was also very good at chess. She would need to think hard and make smart moves if she wanted to win.

Faith learned how to play chess from her dad. He told her the rules and showed her how to play. Chess has many rules.

The game has a queen, knights, rooks, pawns, and others. Faith had to learn the moves each one could make in a game. To play, she had to plan how and when to move each one.

"This tall one is your king," her dad had told her. "You must keep him safe at all times. If I can harm your king, we say he's in check. If you can't save him, it is checkmate, and there is no safe spot for him to move. That's when the game ends."

"I think I get it, Dad," Faith had said. "Can we play now?"

Faith could still picture that first game in her mind. It had ended with her dad saying, "Checkmate! That means I win."

"Let's play again, Dad!" Faith had said.

Faith and her dad played almost every day. Now she played better than he did! Her dad was very proud of her.

Now, Faith played chess for prizes. Often, she would win her matches. Less often, she lost. Sometimes a match ended in a tie. This is called a **draw**.

Faith's last few matches had ended in draws. Today, Faith wanted to win.

"Take your places," a woman said. Faith found her place and took a deep breath.

Faith sat down at the black side. She was playing a boy called Paul. He had white, so he went first. Faith soon saw that Paul was really good at chess.

"Think!" Faith told herself. She made a plan for her next few moves. It worked!

"Checkmate!" Faith said as she reached over to shake Paul's hand.

Story Word Clues

Use the clues to find words in the story.
Write the words.

1. This word tells how Faith feels as she walks into the hall.

2. Dad uses this word to tell about the king.

3. This word tells about a match that ends in a tie.

Story Word Hunt

Learn these words. You will see them in your reading and use them in your writing. Read them to a partner.

done	**there**	**think**	**warm**
went	**without**	**woman**	**worked**

1. Look for each word in a story. Which words were not there?

2. Choose two words. Write sentences using the words.

3. Read the sentences to your partner.

Game Day

by Jia Lee

illustrated by Peter Francis

When it is Game Day, we don't have class. Instead, we will spend this nice warm day outside playing games. That's because Game Day is today!

"Have fun, Rob!" Mom said as she dropped me off on her way to work.

"Don't think about winning," our teacher told us. "Have fun, and be good sports!"

I was on a team with my best pals, Megan and Jay. We like batting, so first we went to hit some balls.

I grabbed a bat and started swinging, but I didn't do too well. I kept missing the ball.

Megan hit well, and so did Jay. Jay's ball went gliding high over the treetops.

I did better at the next game. A small goal sat in the grass. We each got five balls to kick. I kicked one of them so hard that it almost knocked down the goal! I scored all five times.

Jay patted me on the back and said, "You're on fire, Rob!" We all laughed. It was such a good time!

Megan smiled as she walked the beam with a beanbag on her head. She had to get to the end of the beam without letting the beanbag fall. She did it! Go, Megan! Mine fell off after six steps. Jay lost his bag after just two steps!

We laughed and then zipped off to join the crowd for the big race.

We faced the other team and shook
hands with them. Then we were off!

The race began with fast running. Then
we had to go weaving in and out of cones
and hopping in and out of hoops.

My team worked hard, but we didn't win.
I didn't mind. We still had fun. It was fun
racing between cones and through hoops.

A fire truck pulled up when all the games
were done. A smiling face looked at us.

"Who needs to cool off?" the woman
asked, grinning at all of us hot kids.

"Me! Me! I do! I do!" we all yelled.
We danced with joy as the water soaked
us. We giggled and flopped on the grass.
I wish every day could be Game Day!

Story Clues

1. Read the clue.

You kick some of these and hit others.

Who or what is the clue about?

2. Pick something in one of the stories.
Write a clue and read it to a friend.
Can your friend find it?

Blend and Read

1. raw   racing   batted   cawing   salt

2. haul   zipped   fall   scoring   talk

3. prowl   poof   foil   ploy   proud

4. chalky   awful   sprawl   stalk   vault

5. Rob scored all the times he shot at the goal.

6. Megan walked the beam without falling.

My Big Bike Race

by Jia Lee
illustrated by Peter Francis

Do you like riding bikes? I do! I go biking all the time. I use this bike when I ride in the woods.

There are lots of good trails for biking in these woods. One trail has a long hill that's lined with logs. My bike goes skipping and hopping over the logs each time I zip down that hill.

I also race with this bike. I started racing last fall. On each race day, I check my bike to make sure all of its parts are working the way they should be. I test its brakes, pump up its tires, and oil its chain. I fix anything that needs work. These steps help keep me safe in every race.

Last week I had a big race. My mom and dad drove me there. My bike was tied onto the roof of the car. It felt funny to be riding in a car with a bike perched on top of it.

Before we left, I filled my water bottle and crammed all my stuff into my bag. Then I grabbed this hard thing for my head. I never go riding without it!

The race started on the peak of a huge hill. My bike flew down the hill, wheels spinning so fast that clumps of dirt were spitting out on all sides of my tires.

I started braking when I saw the first turn coming up. I didn't brake too hard because I didn't want to start skidding. If I skidded, I could fall, and it hurts to fall off a bike!

The trail weaved into a thicker patch of woods. I zigzagged and bumped my way over rocks and tree roots as I sped down the trail.

My wheels gripped dirt, and I kept my gaze fixed on the steep trail I was flying down. There was no stopping me! I was in the zone!

The trail dipped and turned hard. Then it went up, leading to a ramp jump. I hit the ramp, popped it, and then glided back down to the trail with ease.

I flew past the finish line, beating my best time and clocking in the best time that day. I came in first! My mom was smiling and clapping, and my dad took pictures.

Show What You Know

Reread the four stories to answer these questions.

1. What makes these stories like one another? In what ways do they differ?

2. What do the characters do to get ready for their game or race?

3. How are the characters good sports?

4. What does each character do to get better at his or her sport or game? What could you do to get better at a sport or game?

Talk about the stories with a partner.

Get Started

What sports do you like to watch or play?
Can you name sports that people play
using a ball?

What sports are good for people who like to
run and jump? How can people play ice or
water sports all year long? Read to find out!

Sports Played with a Ball

by Dana Schlein

Do you play soccer or baseball? These games are sports that you play with a ball. Sports are contests. People play games or run races to test their skill and have fun.

Playing sports is good for you. It keeps you fit and helps you grow. It can help your brain grow, too. You find out how to work with others. What sports have you tried?

Soccer is a game played by two teams. People can't use their hands or arms on the ball in soccer, but may use their chests, legs, and feet to move and pass it. They try to get it into the other team's goal to score.

Just one person stands in the goal for each team and may use hands to stop goals. A team that scores more goals wins.

In the U.S.A., football is played using a brown ball that has an odd shape. Teams pass or run with this ball. The other team tries to stop them and get it back.

Teams score if players take the ball past a goal line. Players can kick it through a goal post to score, too. In most other places, **football** is the name people use for **soccer**.

Baseball is a team sport, too. A pitcher tosses a ball over home plate to a person on the other team. That person bats and runs to first base if the ball is hit. People on other bases run, too. The pitching team tries to catch balls or tag people running from base to base. Teams trade places when the batting team makes three outs.

Kickball is a bit like baseball. It has bases that people step on to score points called runs. The other team tries to get them out. Teams trade places after three outs.

A few things in kickball are not the same as in baseball. The ball is bigger and softer, and you don't need a mitt to catch it. It is rolled and kicked, not hit with a bat.

Tennis is a game played by two or four people at a time. To start, one person tosses a small ball and hits it with a racket. It flies over the net, bounces, and a person on the other side tries to hit it back. They hit it back and forth until one misses or can't keep it inside the lines. When a side wins, they all shake hands and say thank you.

Word Ending Hunt

1. Look for words that end in **-es**, **-ing**, or **-ed**. Write the words you find. Count the words you wrote for each ending.

2. Look for spelling changes. Circle the words with a final consonant that was doubled.

3. Use a different color to circle the words with a final **e** that was dropped.

4. Underline the words with no spelling changes before the ending. (Hint: some **-es** words may have an added **-s** and no spelling changes.)

Blend and Read

1. scoring   flipped   hoping   tipping   skies

2. taping   tipped   studied   running   tried

3. sauce   boys   crew   crawl   join

4. retried   untied   unsaved   replayed

5. Have you tried kickball or baseball?

6. Running around the bases is fun!

Sports Played in Water

by Dana Schlein

What do you like to do on hot summer days? Maybe you go swimming. Diving or jumping into cold water helps you keep cool.

Would you swim on cold winter days? Lots of people do! They take part in water sports and train all year long. They need to find places to swim when it's cold out. Many find heated pools for swimming in winter.

To swim, people paddle with their arms and hands and kick with their legs and feet. Those who swim in races may pick just a few kinds of swimming to master for races. One kind of swimming is called the butterfly.

People swim fast in races. They go to swim meets to race. The person with the fastest time wins each race.

People who do diving tell stories of hard dives! They bend, turn, and twist before diving head first into deep water, with their toes pointed and lined up with their arms.

Judges score each dive. Scores are based on how hard each dive is and how it looks. Harder dives get more points than simple ones. The highest score wins.

Some people swim to music as a team. Each person copies the same moves in a way that goes with a song's beat. This kind of team may have up to eight members making moves under water. They hold their breath for a long time, while swimming and kicking or floating in place, all at the same time. It is hard to swim in a group like that.

Rowing boats is fun, but most rowboats do not go too fast. In the sport of rowing, the boats can go quite fast! These racing rowboats are called racing shells. Up to eight can fit in a racing shell.

One person doesn't row, but sits facing the team. That person tells them which way to go and tries to get them to row together.

Surfing is another kind of water sport. It takes place at beaches with big waves. To surf, people ride these big, crashing waves to shore.

First they sit up and paddle with their hands through big waves to get up enough speed to catch a wave. They may lie flat or stand when riding a wave back to the beach.

What Is the Word?

Use the clues to find words in the text.

Clue 1: people paddle and kick to do this

Clue 2: ends in **-ing**

What is the word?

Clue 1: describes rowboats used in races

Clue 2: ends in **-ing**

What is the word?

Now you do it! Give two clues about a text word. Can a partner find the word?

Story Break

1. **Eight** people take **their** places to race.

2. They think about many **things**.

3. Will they be fast **enough** to win?

4. Each one **goes** when they hear "Bang!"

5. They all **move** just as fast as they can.

6. The race is **through,** but who wins?

Pretend you win the race. Write a note to **thank** the other racers and your fans.

Sports Played on Ice

by Dana Schlein

It gets so cold in some places! Lakes and ponds freeze in winter. People who take part in ice sports can train on this ice. It is key to make sure that the ice is thick.

What do people do in places that are not cold enough for ice to form? Can they play ice sports, too? They can train inside ice rinks that stay cold through hot summers.

Ice skating is a fun ice sport. Ice skates are boots with sharp blades on the bottom. Blades let people jump, spin, twirl, and glide on ice. Ice skating is a good way to stay fit.

In some ice sports, people skate to music and get points for fine, fancy foot moves and high jumps. People toss roses onto the icy rink to thank them for skating so well.

In speed skating, people race on an icy track to see who goes the fastest.

In short races, people line up at the starting line. They skate fast, and then the first person to cross the finish line wins.

In long races, two people skate at a time. They skate lap after lap around the track, trying for fast times. The fastest time wins.

What ice sport is this? It's called curling. Curling teams slide large stones on ice. A person slides the big flat stone. Two others sweep in front of it with brooms. The small brush marks on the ice are enough to get the stone to move left or right and speed up or slow down. The key for each team is to get their stone close to the center to win.

Ice hockey is another team sport. People who play hockey use sticks to hit a hard rubber puck while skating. They are smart to use padding and helmets when they play. These things help keep them from getting hurt by hockey sticks, sharp skates, or flying pucks. A team scores when the puck goes past the other team's goalie.

Sleds that go down snowy hills are played with like toys, but bobsleds are not like toys at all! A bobsled has sharp steel blades and can fit two or four people inside.

Bobsleds race down an icy track that twists and turns. The team's chief job is to shift back and forth to move into turns and go faster. Teams with the fastest time win.

Summarize

Think about your reading about sports. Then write to answer these questions.

1. What did you learn about sports played with a ball, water sports, and ice sports? Tell the most important ideas.

2. Did anything you learned about sports surprise you? What was it? Why?

Talk about your answers with a group.

Blend and Read

1. piece   field   sunny   funny   movie

2. alley   brief   fancy   donkey   brownie

3. dried   sliding   cries   skating   dawned

4. shield   jersey   shriek   money   yield

5. The girl goes skating at an ice rink.

6. The sled is sliding down the icy track.

Track and Field

by Dana Schlein

Most kids like to run, toss things, and jump. Running, tossing, and jumping are skills that people use in track and field sports. In track, people run races, or do running and jumping in the same race.

Field sports test jumping and tossing skills. People toss discs and other long pointy things or try to jump very far or high.

Most running contests take place on a track. Each track has four to nine lanes. These races can be short or long, and the key to being on track teams is to run **fast**.

People run fast with quick bursts of speed in short races. In longer races, they may not run as fast, but they must run more laps around the track to finish their races.

Some kinds of track races are run in teams of four. Each person on this team runs part of each race. They take turns running and holding onto a stick. At the end of their part, each one passes this stick to the next person.

It's quite tricky to do, but thrilling to watch! If a stick is dropped, the team is out.

A track race with hurdles tests running and jumping skills. A **hurdle** is like a small fence that people jump over in a race. They must jump all ten hurdles in their lane.

They must be fast and good at jumping to win at hurdles. If their feet or knees knock into a hurdle and make it fall, or if they hit a hurdle with their hands, they will not win.

High jumping is a field contest. You can see a person leap over a thin pole that rests on upright bars. He or she takes a running start and tries to make the highest jump. People jumping get three tries each.

If their feet or legs knock down the pole, they're out. Those who make it over get to try until a person jumps the highest.

(b) ©wavebreakmedia/Shutterstock, (frame) ©Digital Vision/Getty Images

Long jumping tests how far a jump can be. Each person takes a long running start down a runway with a plank at the end. He or she must push off this plank without letting toes cross it. Then it's the jump, with legs pumping as if a person can run through the sky. Judges mark how far each person jumps. The longest jump wins.

Think-Write-Pair-Share

Reread the four texts. Think and then write answers to these questions.

1. Choose two team sports. How are they alike? How are they different?

2. What tools do people use to play some sports? Include examples from different sports in your answer.

3. Which sports in your reading are new to you? Which new sports would you like to try? Why?

Share your work with a partner and then with a group.

Get Started

Have you ever wondered why animals look or act the way they do? Some stories are told to give reasons why things are the way they are.

Why do rabbit tails and possum tails look the way they do? Why do rabbits run fast and stay away from snakes? Read to find out how some storytellers have answered these questions.

Why Rabbits Have Short Tails

based on a Creek/Muscogee tale
illustrated by Katya Longhi

In the past, Rabbit had a long and fluffy tail. He was quite proud of it.

"See my pretty tail?" Rabbit bragged loudly all the time. "Don't you wish you had a tail like mine?"

Fox had a long, fluffy tail, too. He was tired of Rabbit and his endless boasts. So Fox made a plan to trick Rabbit.

Fox knew Rabbit went to the lake every day. First, he waited for the lake to freeze. He cut a hole in the ice, and then he tied four big fish to his tail.

When Fox saw Rabbit, he quickly dropped his tail into the freezing water.

"What are you doing?" Rabbit asked.

"I'm fishing," Fox answered.

"Why are you fishing with your tail?"
Rabbit asked.

"I catch more fish with my tail than with a
hook," said Fox. "In fact, I feel a tug now!"

Fox lifted his tail. Rabbit saw the fish on
Fox's tail. "I need six more fish," Fox said.

"What will you do with all the fish?"
Rabbit asked him.

"I saw a clip with gems on it," said Fox. "I can trade ten fish for it. Bear says there is one clip left. I'm going to put it on my tail to make it sparkle. I'll come back again and fish until I have ten fish to trade."

Fox left Rabbit on the ice and went to hide in the woods. He waited to see what Rabbit would do.

"I won't let his tail look better than mine!" Rabbit said. "I need that clip! I'll stay here all night and catch ten fish," Rabbit said, and he stuck his tail into the fishing hole.

Fox came back at sunrise and asked Rabbit what he was doing. Rabbit was so cold he could hardly talk.

"Fishing," he said weakly.

"Did you catch any fish?" Fox asked.

Rabbit tried to look, but the hole was
frozen again and he was stuck!

"Let me help," Fox said as he gave Rabbit
a mighty push.

"Ouch!" yelped Rabbit. His long tail was
stuck in the ice, and a fuzzy ball was in its
place. To this day, rabbits have short tails.

Story Word Clues

Read each set of clues. Find the correct word in the story.

1. I end with **-less**. I tell about Rabbit's bragging. What word am I?

2. I end with **-ly**. I tell how Rabbit spoke when his tail was stuck in the ice. What word am I?

3. I end with **-y**. I tell about Rabbit's tail at the end of the story. What word am I?

Blend and Read

1. fluffy   hopeful   tricky   hopeless

2. sadly   harmless   quickly   harmful

3. tapping   taping   tidying   tidied

4. happily   wonderful   beautiful

5. Rabbit boasts about his fluffy tail.

6. Rabbit answers Fox weakly.

Why Possums Have Furless Tails

based on a Cherokee tale
illustrated by Katya Longhi

Possum sat on his porch. He brushed his long, black, silky tail. That tail was his pride and joy.

"Look at my fine tail," he said to Rabbit. "I will be at the meeting tonight, sitting where everyone can see my tail. Fox says his tail is fine, but mine is so much better."

"Possum is too boastful," Rabbit said to himself. "He does not need to brag about his tail all the time. He makes me miss my old tail too much."

To Possum, Rabbit said, "Your tail must look its best for the meeting. I will send someone to brush and trim it. Please, don't thank me. It gives me joy to help you."

Soon, Insect came to see Possum. She
had a nice smile and sharp claws.

"I am Insect," she said. "Rabbit sent me
to brush and trim your silky long tail."

Possum lay down. He felt the brush on
his tail and heard a snipping sound.

"Insect does that well," Possum said to
himself, and he quickly went to sleep.

"Wake up, Possum," said Insect. "Your tail is done. I gave it a new look. This ribbon holds it all in place. Do not take it off at the meeting until the drumming starts."

That night, Possum held his head high as he walked into the meeting space.

"My tail is so fine," he said to himself. "That's why they're all giving me looks."

At last, the drums began to beat. Possum got up. Slowly, he took the ribbon from around his tail and held his tail above his head for all to see.

"Look at my fine tail!" he sang loudly. "It is so graceful and smooth!"

The animals laughed and pointed at Possum. This puzzled Possum.

Then Possum took a look at his tail. All
he saw was a long, bald thing with scales!
Possum also saw Rabbit holding the ribbon
with a pile of black fur at his side.

Possum fell to the ground and hid his
face. He stayed like that until all the animals
had left. And to this day, possums have
furless tails.

Read It, Change It

Read each word and follow the directions to write a new word. Hint: You may have to add or take away letters.

1. furless   Change **-less** to **-y**.

2. slowly   Change **slow** to **quick**.

3. graceful   Change **-ful** to **-less**.

4. loudly   Change **loud** to **soft**.

5. perfect   Add **-ly**.

Check your work with a partner. Take turns using the new words in sentences.

Secret Word Game

 Play with a partner.
Use a timer. Take turns.

above	again	around	does
gives	live	says	what

1. Think of a word in the box.

2. Set the timer.

3. Tell a clue about the word.

4. Your partner tries to guess the secret word.

5. Continue until your partner guesses or time runs out.

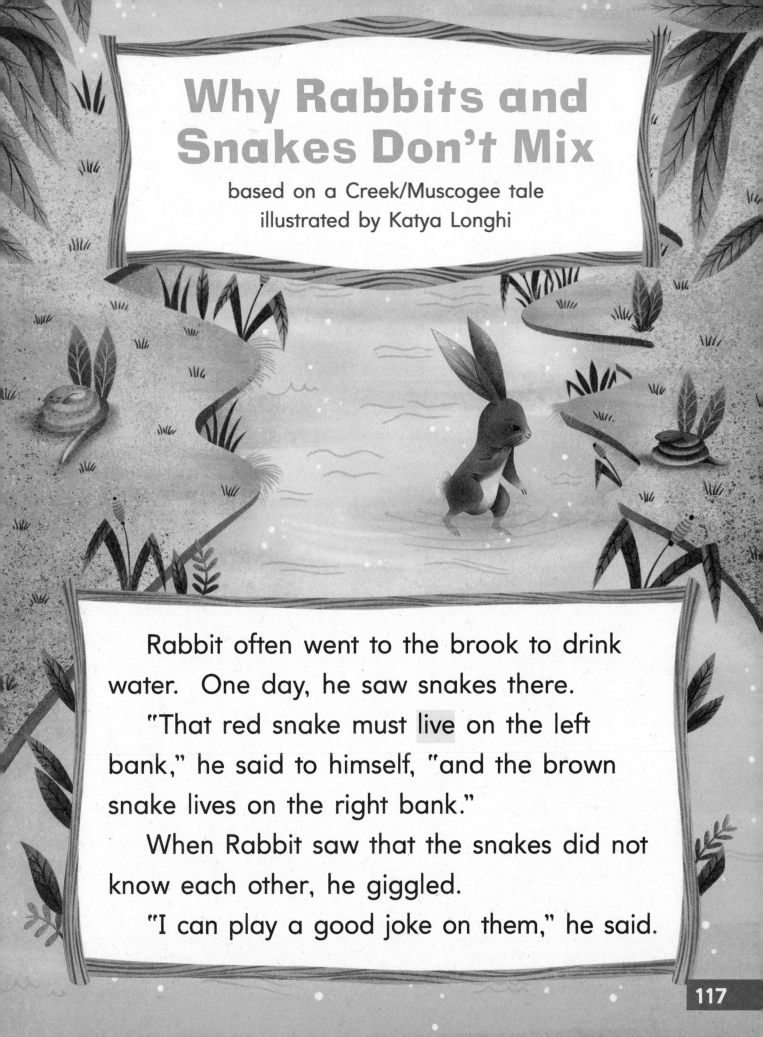

Why Rabbits and Snakes Don't Mix

based on a Creek/Muscogee tale
illustrated by Katya Longhi

Rabbit often went to the brook to drink water. One day, he saw snakes there.

"That red snake must live on the left bank," he said to himself, "and the brown snake lives on the right bank."

When Rabbit saw that the snakes did not know each other, he giggled.

"I can play a good joke on them," he said.

Rabbit hopped to the left bank and told the red snake, "I bet I can tug you right out of this brook."

"You can't. You are small and weak!" the red snake said. "I won't budge an inch."

"Let's have a contest then," Rabbit said. "I will get a long vine. We can each take an end. We will see who can tug the hardest."

Rabbit swam to the right bank. He set up
the same contest with the brown snake. Then
Rabbit got a vine. He returned to the left
bank and gave an end of the vine to the
red snake.

"I'm going to swim to the right bank,"
Rabbit called. "When I get there, I'll give
a yell. That's the sign to start tugging."

Rabbit gave the other end to the brown snake. He restated the rules for that snake. Then he hopped off to sit under a big tree to see what would happen next.

"Tug!" Rabbit yelled. "Tug now!"

Both snakes leaned back and tugged with all their might.

Rabbit sat back to watch them tug.

"Wow," said the red snake. "Rabbit is not as weak as he looks!"

"How can that small rabbit tug so hard?" the brown snake asked.

The snakes kept tugging. Rabbit snorted.

"What was that sound?" each snake asked. Both snakes swam into the brook to find out what had made that snorting sound.

When they saw each other, the snakes gasped. They knew that Rabbit had tricked them, and they got very mad at him.

"You tricked us, Rabbit!" hissed the red snake. "That was unwise. You may not drink at this brook again! If you do, we will both bite you!" And to this day, rabbits stay away from snakes.

Characters

Think about the characters and how they act.

Fox

Rabbit

Possum

Write two things you learned about each character. Then choose one character and write a question you would like to ask the character.

Share your work with a partner or a group.

Blend and Read

1. stuffy   unlock   reuse   unhelpful

2. unload   retie   meanly   priceless

3. found   spoil   always   ground

4. review   unlikely   refinish   unready

5. The red snake says Rabbit is unwise.

6. Was Rabbit's silly trick unkind?

Why Rabbits Run Fast

based on a Creek/Muscogee tale
illustrated by Katya Longhi

"I take big leaps. I have big feet," sang Rabbit. "I am so fast. I can't be beat!"

Rabbit hopped around and sang his boast again. He repeated it so loudly that it woke Turtle up from her nap.

"Hi, slowpoke," said Rabbit.

"That's unkind, Rabbit," said Turtle.

"Yes, it's true!" said Rabbit, laughing.

"I am faster than you think," said Turtle in a huff. Rabbit just laughed harder.

"Let's race then," Rabbit said. "Meet me here at noon. We can race over these two hills to the big rock above the town."

"I'll see you then, Rabbit!" said Turtle. Rabbit hopped into the woods.

"That was pretty brainless," Turtle said to herself. "I need help to win this race and stop Rabbit from his pointless bragging."

Turtle needed a plan. She stumped off to find her mom and dad. Together, they hatched up a plan.

At noon, Rabbit and Turtle met. The race began. Rabbit dashed over the first big hill.

When he reached the hilltop, he saw a turtle racing down the other side! Rabbit ran faster. He saw the turtle reach the top of the next hill.

Then Rabbit reached the next hilltop. "I will beat that turtle now," he said, puffing hard. "I am the fastest. I have to win!"

Just then, he saw a turtle zipping down the second hill!

"How can this be?" Rabbit asked. "How can that slowpoke be beating me?" He zoomed down the hill, but it was no use.

The turtle reached the end first. All the animals clapped and cheered as Rabbit flopped to the ground in a heap.

"I feel unwell," he moaned.

"Well, you did your best," said the turtle.

How did Turtle win the race? It was a trick! Turtle's mom and dad hid beside the path of the race. Then they popped up as Rabbit came over each hill. All this time, Turtle had stayed back at the starting line.

Turtle stumped back home to return to her nap. Rabbit never found out about Turtle's trick. And to this day, rabbits run fast.

What If?

Reread the four stories. Then answer the questions.

1. What if Rabbit did not brag or play tricks on others? How might the stories be different?

2. What if Fox, Rabbit, and Possum were less proud of their tails or the two snakes knew each other?

3. What if Rabbit didn't wake up Turtle? What would change in the last story?

Talk about your answers with a partner.

Get Started

What do you know about water? What animals live in or near water? In what ways do people use water? Why is water so important?

Read to find out!

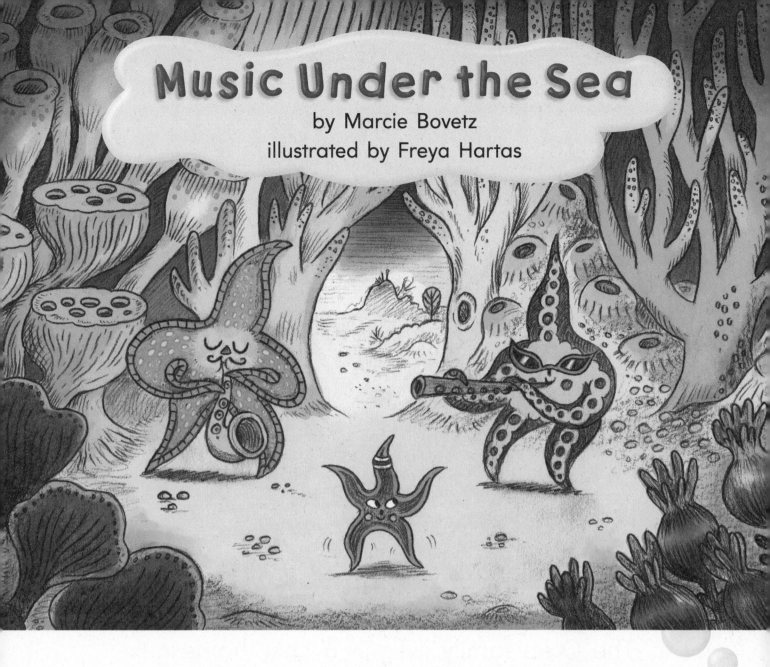

Music Under the Sea

by Marcie Bovetz

illustrated by Freya Hartas

The Star family lives under the water in a cozy home. Mom Star likes to play her flute. Dad Star likes to play his horn. They make jazz music day and night.

The Stars have a baby. Her name is Tulip, and she likes loud songs, too. She taps her feet to the jazzy beat.

The Crab family lives in a cozy home next to the Stars. Mom Crab likes to play her harp. She plays slowly and sweetly. Dad Crab sings in a low voice. They like slow, sweet songs instead of loud songs.

Their baby is named Clover. She also likes these slow, sweet songs that her mom and dad play at home.

One night, the Stars played very loud music. Mom Crab, Dad Crab, and Clover could not sleep at all.

"Just once, I would like to relax at bedtime!" Mom Crab cried out.

"We'll ask them to stop," Dad Crab said. "I hope they will delay playing their music until morning, so we can sleep tonight."

The Crabs marched over to the Star family's home. Mom Crab knocked loudly, but the Stars kept right on playing. Mom Crab knocked again, even louder.

The music stopped, and the door swung open at once. Dad Star smiled at them.

"Hi! Come on in!" he said brightly. "We're so glad to see you!"

"We came to tell you that the music is a bit too loud," Dad Crab replied. "I don't mean to be unkind, but we need to sleep."

"Sure!" Dad Star cried. "That's fine. We'll tone it down now, but please come back in the morning, so we can all play sweet, smooth jazz together. Sleep well!"

"That sounds good!" said Mom Crab.

Now the Stars and the Crabs play songs together in a band called the Sea Scales. They hold concerts in parks and play at picnics. The animals who hear them like them to play and replay their best songs.

Tulip and Clover sing with the band, too. They tap their feet and sway to the sweet sounds of music under the sea.

What Is the Word?

Use the clues to find words in the story.
Write the words.

Clue 1: what the Crabs want to do at night

Clue 2: rhymes with **Max**

What is the word?

Clue 1: how the Stars' door swings

Clue 2: rhymes with **Ben**

What is the word?

Now you do it! Give two clues about a story word. Can a partner find the word?

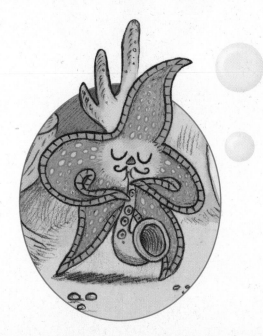

Blend and Read

1. pony   baby   cozy   lazy   over

2. pilot   diver   fever   tidy   even

3. chief   funny   thief   furry   niece

4. sofa   table   soda   able   local

5. Do the Stars like to play music loudly?

6. The band replays songs for their fans.

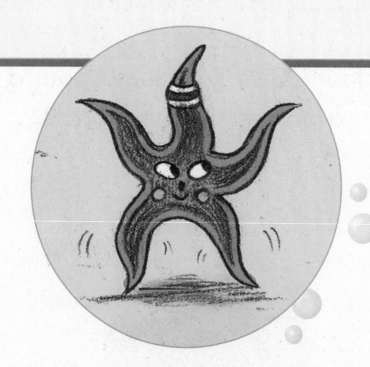

We Need Water
by Marcie Bovetz

A globe shows what our world looks like. If you look at one, you can see how much is blue. The blue on the globe is water.

Our world has much more water than land. You can find water in the sea and in lakes, ponds, rivers, and creeks. Water can be in small puddles or huge lakes. It is all around us.

Water takes different forms. It falls down from the sky as drops of rain and also as hail, sleet, or snow. It runs into creeks and rivers. It flows into lakes and into the sea.

Water can become a gas and rise back up into the sky. The water droplets join and form clouds. Then they will fall down to our world again as rain, sleet, snow, or ice.

All living things need water. Plants need it to grow. Plants use their roots to get water. The roots go down into the ground and take in water from the ground.

Like plants, animals need water. Wild animals find it in ponds, lakes, and creeks. Birds drink from puddles or birdbaths. Cows and sheep drink fresh water from big tubs.

Humans need water, too. Pipes bring clean water into homes.

How do you use water? You need it for taking baths and to wash your hands. You need it for keeping teeth clean. You need it for cooking. You need to drink it to stay in good shape.

Do you add ice cubes to drinks to make them cold? Ice is just frozen water!

Some people do not have clean water that comes from pipes. They must go to pumps or wells to get water. Then they lug it home in pails or bottles.

People who live in dry lands with just a little water might hike for miles to get to it. Then every last drop must be used. Water is like gold in these dry lands.

It is good to use water wisely. Do not let it run down the drain for a long time when you brush your teeth. Try not to waste water. You can also catch rain in buckets and use it to help garden plants grow.

You can pick up trash to keep creeks and lakes clean or help clean up beaches. We can all help protect water in our world.

Word Clues

Read each set of clues. Find the correct word in the text. Write it.

1. Ice is water that has been ____.
    What is the word?

2. This word tells what happens to water when it changes to a gas. What is the word?

3. When we help keep water safe and clean, we do this to the water. What is the word?

Use That Word

Take turns. Play with a friend until you use all the words.

these	they	once	people
wash	water	who	world

1. Pick a word and read it.

2. Your friend uses the word in a sentence.

3. Then your friend picks a word and reads it.

4. You use your friend's word in a sentence.

Jobs That Use Water

by Marcie Bovetz

Did you ever help wash cars? Some people's job is to wash cars. They use soapy water and hoses to get cars clean. Clean cars look super on a sunny day!

Some people's job is washing dishes, pots, and pans. They use lots of hot, soapy water. We need clean dishes for eating and clean pots and pans for cooking.

Farming is another job that uses water. Farmers must water crops that cannot grow without water. Farms can't grow plums, peaches, corn, wheat, or other foods without it.

Cows, sheep, goats, hens, and other farm animals need water to drink. Cows and goats cannot make milk without it.

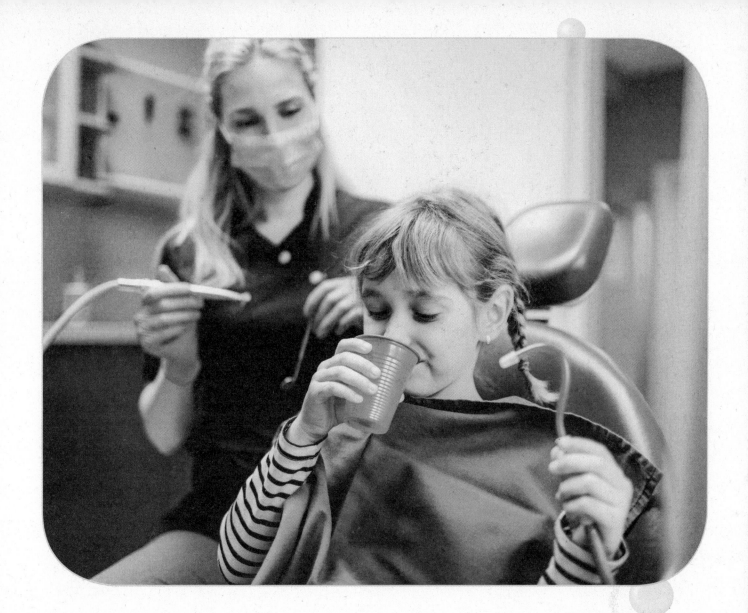

People use water to do jobs that help us stay well. Moms, dads, and nurses wash out our cuts with soap and water to get rid of germs. Dentists use water when they check and clean our teeth.

Some people teach kids how to swim. They watch over kids swimming in pools or lakes and jump in to help if it is needed.

Some jobs are on boats that go far out to sea. Fishing boats catch fish with nets and long fishing lines. Big ships bring fish and other things to markets for people to buy.

Some boats take cars on short trips over water. These boats help people cross water and still use their cars when they reach land. It's fun to be in a car on a boat.

Some people in the Armed Forces work on big ships. Some may dive under the water. Some are pilots who fly over blue waves in jets. These pilots fly jets right off a ship at sea and land back on it, too.

Many people in the Armed Forces sail on ships all over the world and help keep us safe.

Artists use water to make all kinds of art. It can be added to paints. Artists mix paints to make new colors. They mix clay with water to make vases, cups, or dishes.

You can mix paper and glue with water, too, and shape it into things. After letting them dry, you can paint them.

How might you use water to make art?

K-W-L Chart

Think about your reading. Then make a chart like the one below to show what you have learned about water.

Water		
K	**W**	**L**
What I **K**now	What I **W**ant to Know	What I **L**earned

Talk about your work in a group.

Blend and Read

1. spider   human   tiger   music   student

2. recess   open   relax   over   robot

3. blue   bloom   clue   cool   true

4. rotate   tuba   silent   siren   decode

5. Some pilots can fly jets off a huge ship.

6. These workers do a super job every day!

Car Wash

by Marcie Bovetz
illustrated by Macky Pamintuan

A car can't fit in a bathtub, but you can still wash it. How can you get a car clean?

My dad and I take our dirty car to the car wash. That's a place for cleaning cars. The car goes in with mud and grime on it, and it comes out bright and clean!

This car wash is open. We can drive right into it. We must stay inside the car and keep all the windows shut.

The car rides on a track that moves. Water jets get it all wet. Next, soap shoots out to clean off the grime. Then more water washes off the soap. All clean!

This is another kind of car wash. It has people who clean the dirty cars. They use soap and water and rub the cars to get off all the dust and dirt. Then they dry them off by hand using soft, clean cloths.

Dirty water and soap go down drains into tanks. Doing this helps keep rivers and lakes clean.

Another kind of car wash is called a self-wash. That means we can do the washing. We drop coins in slots to pay for it. We follow steps in this kind of car wash.

I use a hose to shoot water at my dad's car. After that, we swirl on soap and get the car all soapy. Last, I soak the car with more water to get it clean. I did a good job!

People can wash cars at home, too. We need water, a hose, soap, and pails. We also need clean rags or cloths.

Water flows and soap swirls. Rags and cloths swoop in to dry. Last, we rub all the windows clean. See that nice shine?

We wash the car in my yard on the grass so that the water will soak into the ground.

What about vans, trucks, and buses?
These big rigs get dirty, too. How can they
get clean?

Big rigs need a big space for washing.
Places for cleaning big trucks have huge
spaces and huge hoses.

Look at cars and trucks that drive past
you. Can you spot the clean ones?

Think-Draw-Pair-Share

Reread the four texts. Think and then draw to answer these questions.

1. What are some jobs that use water? Draw a job that you would like to do. How would you use water for that job?

2. What are some ways people use water? How did you use water today?

Share your work with a partner and then in a group.

Get Started

How do some animals use their claws? Why do animals have different kinds of teeth? How do animals with horns use their horns? How can pointy spines help an animal? Read to find out!

Claws Swipe

by Myra Blake

People have flat nails on the tips of their fingers and toes. Many animals have claws instead. Claws may be long or short and can also be quite sharp.

Different animals use their claws to do different things. Claws can help an animal get food. An owl can grab snakes, rabbits, mice, or other small animals with its claws.

A black bear uses its claws to get food. It digs up roots and rips into logs with its claws to get at insects and grubs. It uses its claws to dig into ant nests, too. Those ants look yummy to the bear.

A bear digs into the bark of trees with its claws to mark off for other bears the space it thinks of as its home.

Some animals use their claws to dig. A mole digs tunnels and makes its nest underground where it is dark and cool. It digs in soil to find beetles, grubs, and other bugs to eat. It won't take too long!

Moles do not see well, but they are one of the fastest kinds of animals for digging. A mole can dig faster than many animals.

Animals may also use their claws to hold things, cling to things, or hang in trees. The sloth's claws are shaped like hooks. It hooks its claws on branches, hangs upside down, and eats leaves.

It moves slowly from tree to tree in this way. It is so slow moss can grow on it! It is one of the slowest animals in the world.

A house cat can defend itself with its claws. It will swipe its sharp claws at a dog if the dog gets too close. Those claws could really hurt a dog. Cats that hunt depend on their sharp claws, too.

A cat's claws stay inside its paw pads almost all the time. The cat pops them out when it needs them.

Some animals use their claws to clean, or groom, their fur. Can you see this one grooming its pal's fur? It uses its claws to clean out yucky stuff that gets stuck in the fur on its pal's back.

Claws also come in handy if an animal has an itch. Claws can be quite useful for animals that have them!

Hunt for Words That Compare

1. Look in **Claws Swipe** for words that end with **-er** and **-est**. Write each word you find.

2. Work with a partner. Talk about the things that the **-er** and **-est** words compare.

3. Think of other words with **-er** or **-est** you could use to compare animals.

Blend and Read

1. finest   lower   lightest   thinner   quickest

2. nicest   wilder   neater   wetter   sweetest

3. undo   replay   unwind   redo   unkind

4. silliest   crazier   funnier   sleepiest

5. Which animal digs the fastest?

6. Are claws sharper than your fingernails?

Teeth Chomp
by Myra Blake

© Christian Vinces/Shutterstock

 Smile! You have teeth to use for eating food. Animals use their teeth to eat, too. Animal teeth come in different shapes and sizes for eating different kinds of food.

 What animal has the sharpest teeth? This fish could win that prize! Its teeth help it eat insects, frogs, other fish, and even dead animals it finds in rivers where it lives.

Some animals have long, sharp teeth called fangs. This animal can live in plains, grasslands, forests, and other spaces. It uses its fangs to catch and eat animals.

It has smaller teeth behind its fangs that can crush bones. Yes, it can eat bones! It has other, sharper teeth that slice and cut meat into pieces small enough for it to eat.

A beaver uses its sharp front teeth to chop down trees. It carries them in its teeth and uses them to make dams. The dam makes a pond where the beaver lives.

Beaver teeth get dull from chewing on so much wood, which would not be helpful for the beaver. It should be glad that its teeth never stop growing and always stay sharp!

Most animals that eat plants have flat, wide teeth. This animal has sharp teeth in front for nipping and pulling up the grass it eats. Its back teeth look like bumpy stones. Those are the teeth that grind the grass.

Did you know that a cow has no top front teeth? Instead, it has a thick pad that its lower front teeth press as it pulls up grass.

This animal has large front teeth called tusks. It can push down trees with them so it can reach the parts it wants to eat. It digs up grass and plant roots with its tusks and uses the tusks to dig for water.

Tusks can be many feet long. Males have the longest tusks. How would you use tusks if you had them?

Look at all those teeth! A gator has lots
and lots of teeth, but it does not use them
for chewing. It uses them to grab and hold
the animals it eats.

It bites a big animal and shakes it into
smaller bits before eating it, and it can eat
small animals in one gulp. New teeth grow
in to replace its old ones all the time.

Read It, Change It

Read each word. Then follow the directions to write a new word. Read each new word.

1. **lower**   Change **er** to **est**.

2. **sharpest**   Change **est** to **er**.

3. **longest**   Change **est** to **er**.

4. **smaller**   Change **er** to **est**.

Check your work with a partner. Take turns using the new words in sentences.

Sentence Starters

Knowing how to read and write these words can make you a better reader and writer. Read the words to a partner.

animal	could	different	pull
should	talk	won't	would

Use the sentence starters to tell your partner about your reading.

1. Some **animals** use their claws to _____.

2. **Animals** have **different** kinds of _____.

3. An **animal could** use tusks to _____.

Then tell about animal claws and teeth.

Horns Help
by Myra Blake

Animals that eat only plants do not have big fangs for biting, but some of them have horns. Their horns help protect them from the animals that eat meat.

An animal with horns can use them to jab and poke at big cats or other animals that hunt. If it could talk, it would say, "Go away! I won't let you catch me!"

This is a bighorn sheep. It is named for the big, curled horns on the male sheep, called rams. Rams bash horns with other rams to sort out who is the top ram.

Female sheep have shorter horns. Male and female bighorns use their horns to rub the spines off cactuses. Then the bighorns can eat cactuses without getting jabbed.

These goats live high up on hills. The male goat is called a billy and has sharp black horns. He uses his horns to battle other billies at times. The male billy goats have thicker horns than female goats.

A baby goat is called a kid. Kids have bumps called horn buds on their heads. These horn buds will grow into horns.

This big animal has horns that are a bit like spikes. It can use its horns to poke animals that try to hunt it and make the hunting animals go away.

These shaggy beasts rub their horns on pine trees or other trees with bark that gives off a smell. This habit may help keep away insects that pester them.

This animal has horns on top of its nose! Its horns are different from cow, sheep, or goat horns. Those animals have bone in their horns.

The horn on this animal has no bone in it. It is made of the same stuff as the nails on your fingers and toes. It uses its horn for digging, defending itself, and for playing.

Are the things on this elk's head horns?
No. An elk has antlers. Antlers are made
of bone. Antlers are not the same as horns.
When it gets warmer, elk shed their antlers
and grow new ones that have soft fuzz on
them that's called velvet.

Animals with horns don't shed them and
grow new ones, unlike animals with antlers.

Compare and Contrast

Use details from your reading to write answers to the questions below.

1. How are claws, horns, and teeth alike?

2. In what ways can animal teeth be different? How do animals use different kinds of teeth?

3. Study the photos in one text. How are the teeth, horns, or claws of the animals different or alike? In what other ways are the animals alike or different?

Discuss your answers with a group.

Blend and Read

1. stories   silly   sillier   funny   funnier

2. trying   saving   sobbed   saved   tried

3. poem   open   human   over   even

4. easier   hazier   simpler   friendliest

5. A kid's horn buds will get bigger.

6. Beaver teeth are made for chomping.

Spines Jab

by Myra Blake

Ouch! Have you ever been poked by a thorn? Then you should know how useful having sharp points could be for an animal.

This sea animal has spines on its back. The spines help keep it safe from fish, turtles, and other sea animals that would like to eat it.

Sea urchins have spines, too. If a fish could talk, it might say, "I should go find something less sharp to eat." Yet many fish are glad to gobble sea urchins. Birds, otters, and crabs eat them, too.

Sea urchins can jam into cracks between rocks. Their spines help hold them in place so animals can't pull them out.

What would this fish say if it could talk? It might say, "Boo!" Its spines lie flat when it is swimming and pop up when an animal starts coming close to it.

Then the fish puffs itself up into a big ball with spikes sticking out. Puffing up gives the other animal a fright and makes the fish hard for the animal to grab and eat.

This reptile has prickles that look like horns. An animal that picks it up is jabbed by these prickles. The reptile may be dropped quickly! Then it has time to run and hide.

The reptile's skin colors also help it blend in with the sand and dirt where it lives. That helps keep it safe, too.

This hedgehog has very sharp spines poking out from its head to its tail. Animals that try to grab it are sure to get jabbed.

A hedgehog can roll itself into a ball. It tucks in its head, feet, and belly and leaves its pointy spines sticking out. Few animals would want to bite such a prickly snack!

This animal has long spines called quills. It starts shaking and rattling its quills when an animal comes too close.

It lashes its tail at the other animal so that its quills stick into the other animal's skin. An animal that gets poked by this animal's quills won't be likely to hunt for it again!

Turn and Talk

Reread the four texts. Then answer these questions.

1. How do claws and horns help the animals that have them?

2. Why do animals have teeth that are different shapes and sizes?

3. How can an animal's spikes help it stay safe? How else do its spikes help it?

Turn and talk about your answers with a partner.

MODULE 11 ■ WEEK 1

= High-Frequency Word

BOOK 1 A Place to Eat p. 5

■ **Decodable Words**

TARGET SKILL: *Vowel Diphthongs ow, ou*

blouses, count, crowds, down*, found*, frowned, gown, how*, loud, now*, out*, sounds, town, wow

PREVIOUSLY TAUGHT SKILLS

an*, and*, art, as*, be*, beep, before*, big*, bikes, blue*, books*, bookstore, buses, but*, by*, cabs, can*, can't*, cars*, cell, crack, curb, dad, don't*, drive, eat*, far*, fast*, fell*, find*, follow*, food*, for*, get*, go*, good*, Grace, had*, hand*, hanging, he*, help*, his*, hope, huge, I*, I'm*, if*, in*, into*, is*, it*, just*, know*, leading, led, left*, let's*, like*, look*, looked*, looks*, make*, map, maps, me*, means, mom, much*, my*, name*, needed*, new*, next*, no*, nose, noses, objects, off*, old*, on*, or*, paintings, pass*, past, peek, perfect, place*, racks, red*, scarf, see*, sells, shop*, show*, sign, sings*, sit*, smell, sniff, so*, start*, started*, step, stop*, store, such*, tells*, that*, that's, them*, these*, this*, tilting, time*, to*, told, too*, trip, trucks, us*, use*, way*, we*, well*, while*, will*, window*, with*, yellow*, zoom

■ **High-Frequency Words**

REVIEW

answer, pointed, right, voice, walk, watch, where

PREVIOUSLY TAUGHT

a, air, all, are, could, from, here, hurry, many, of, our, people, pretty, said, says, something, the, there, through, wasn't, working, would

BOOK 2 At the Park p. 13

■ **Decodable Words**

TARGET SKILL: *Vowel Diphthongs ow, ou*

counted, crowd, down*, ground*, hometown, how*, howling, louder, sound, sounded, sounds, town, wow

PREVIOUSLY TAUGHT SKILLS

after*, and*, as*, at*, band, be*, beat, before*, bending, big*, blast, booming, brakes, button, came*, cars*, clap, dad, dance, dark, deep, did*, do*, doing*, drop, ease, fast*, faster, feet, few*, flashed, flights, flips, for*, free, fun*, get*, girl*, glide, go*, going*, good*, got*, green*, had*, hands*, hat, he*, head*, held*, her*, his*, I*, ice, in*, into*, is*, it*, jumping*, just*, keep*, know*, let*, let's*, lights, like*, looked*, lush, man*, maybe*, miss*, mom, much*, my*, new*, not*, off*, on*, park, part, past, place*, pressed, rocked*, rolling, rubber, run*, saying*, see*, seemed, she*, show*, sighed, sing* slick, slid, smile, songs, soon*, sped, spin, started*, starting*, steep, steps, stick, still*, stop*, stops*, subway, such*, take*, tap, than*, that*, that's*, them*, then*, things*, this*, to*, top, tracks, train, trains, trip, trucks, tunnels, turning*, up*, us*, wait*, waited*, way*, we*, went*, when*, while*, will*, window*, with*, zoomed

■ **High-Frequency Words**

REVIEW

right, voice, walked, walking, watched, watching, where

PREVIOUSLY TAUGHT

a, above, all could, hear, heard, money, never, of, our, people, said, saw, the, through, together, was, wasn't, were, would

BOOK 3 **Good Catch, Kid** p. 21

■ Decodable Words

TARGET SKILLS: *Vowel Diphthongs ow, ou; oi, oy*
batboy, boy*, cowboy, crowd, down*, foil, found*, joined*, loud, now*, out*, pointed*, Roy, wow

PREVIOUSLY TAUGHT SKILLS

and*, as*, asked*, at*, bat, be*, big*, bit, bite, blue*, but*, came*, can*, catch, Clark, dad, dad's, didn't*, do*, dog, drinks, eat*, ended*, far*, few*, first*, fly*, followed*, food*, for*, game, gate, gave*, get*, go*, going*, good*, got*, grin, had*, hand*, handed*, hands*, hard*, he*, him*, his*, hit*, home*, hot*, I*, in*, inside*, is*, it*, jumped*, keep*, kid, landed*, last, left*, let's*, like*, line*, little*, long*, looked*, made*, man*, me*, missed*, mom, more*, my*, name*, next*, nice, off*, on*, paid, park, peeled, pen, pitch, plate, play*, prize, railing, reached*, road, sat*, saying*, seats, see*, shirt, smelled, smile, snacks, so*, soon*, spoke, stand, stands, still*, stood, store, stub, swung, tell*, ten, that*, then*, things*, this*, ticket, time*, to*, told, too*, took*, turns*, up*, us*, wait*, waited*, way*, we*, went*, wide, will*, with*, yay, yelled, you*, you'll*, yum

■ High-Frequency Words

REVIEW

answer, answered, pointed, right, voice, walked, watch, watched, where, write

PREVIOUSLY TAUGHT

a, again, always, are, could, couldn't, heard, many, of, our, said, the, there, there's, very, was, were, would

BOOK 4 **Going Up** p. 29

■ Decodable Words

TARGET SKILLS: *Vowel Diphthongs ow, ou; oi, oy*
boy*, coin, down*, out*, outside, pointing*, points*, mouth, now*, Roy, town, toy

PREVIOUSLY TAUGHT SKILLS

added, and*, ants, as*, ask*, asks*, at*, before*, bench, best*, birds*, blink, bookstore, both*, breeze, button, by*, can*, cars*, cats, Clark, crane, dad, day*, did*, do*, don't*, drop, far*, feels*, fit, for*, force, forget, fun*, game, garden, get*, gets*, girl*, glide, go*, going*, hands*, hang, hat, he*, head*, her*, high*, him*, hold*, holds*, holes, home*, I*, if*, in*, into*, is*, it*, it's*, just*, last, late, ledge, let's*, lights, like*, little*, look*, looks*, lot*, make*, man*, me*, mom, more*, much*, my*, nap, neck, new*, no*, nods, notebook, on*, park, peer, place*, planting*, please*, presses, resting, rooftop, say*, see*, seeds, set*, shop*, shut, slot, smiles, so*, start*, starting*, step, stop*, sun*, tell*, tells*, thanks, them*, then*, thing*, things*, think*, this*, time*, to*, today*, top, trip, up*, us*, way*, we*, we're*, when*, whips, whisks, will*, windows*, with*, yes*, you*, zoom

■ High-Frequency Words

REVIEW

answer, pointing, points, right, voice, want, was, watch, where, write

PREVIOUSLY TAUGHT

a, about, are, because, call, doors, even, eyes, have, hear, here, near, of, one, our, people, says, story, the, there, through, two, very, words, your

= High-Frequency Word

BOOK 1 Time to Train p. 37

■ Decodable Words

TARGET SKILL: *Vowel Patterns: /ô/*

all*, always*, ball*, called*, calls*, chalk, dawn, fall*, hall, launches, Shawn, taut, vault, walks*

PREVIOUSLY TAUGHT SKILLS

and*, arms, as*, asks*, at*, bag, bar, bed*, before*, bend, bends, big*, bottle, butter, car*, claps, coach, dad, dashes, down*, dresses, drive, each* eat*, eggs, feet, flips, food*, for*, get*, gets*, go*, good*, grabs, grip, grips, hands*, hang, hard*, he*, helps*, high*, higher, him*, himself*, his*, hold*, holding*, hop, horse*, in*, into*, is*, it*, it's*, jam, job, jump*, jumps*, keeping*, knows*, lands*, last, legs, let's*, lifts, like*, long*, makes*, milk, nice, not*, now*, off*, on*, or*, out*, peanut, reaches*, rings, rubs, runs*, same*, sees*, serves, set*, slap, slip, so*, solid, start*, still*, straps, strides, swings, takes*, thanks*, that*, them*, then*, thing*, this*, time*, to*, toast, today*, too*, town, train, training, trying*, turns*, twirls, twists, up*, upside, waist, way*, weekend, well*, when*, will*, with*, you*

■ High-Frequency Words

REVIEW

done, there, warm, warms, woman, work, worked, works

PREVIOUSLY TAUGHT

a, air, are, around, many, of, one, only, other, over, people, pulls, pushes, puts, says, the, they, together, was, water, what, where

BOOK 2 Faith Plays Chess p. 45

■ Decodable Words

TARGET SKILL: *Vowel Patterns: /ô/*

all*, almost*, also*, called*, draw*, draws*, hall, Paul, pawns, saw, small*, talking*, tall, walking*

PREVIOUSLY TAUGHT SKILLS

and*, as*, at*, better*, big*, bit, black, boy*, breath, but*, can*, can't*, check, checkmate, chess, dad, day*, deep, did*, down*, each*, ended, ends*, Faith, Faith's, felt*, few*, first*, for*, found*, game, get*, good*, had*, hand*, hard*, harm, has*, he*, he's, her*, herself*, him*, how*, I*, if*, in*, into*, is*, it*, keep*, kid, kids, king, knew*, knights, last, less, let's*, lip, lost, made*, make*, match, matches, means, mind*, must*, need*, next*, no*, now*, place*, places*, plan*, play*, played*, playing*, plays*, prizes, proud, queen, reached*, rooks, rules, safe, sat*, save, say*, saying*, shake, she*, showed*, side*, smart, so*, soon*, spot, still*, take*, than*, that*, that's*, this*, tie, times*, to*, today*, told, took*, we*, when*, white*, win, with*, you*

■ High-Frequency Words

REVIEW

there, think, went, woman, worked

PREVIOUSLY TAUGHT

a, again, could, every, from, full, here, learn, learned, many, move, moves, of, often, one, others, over, picture, really, said, sometimes, the, very, wanted, was, would, your

MODULE 11 ■ WEEK 2

BOOK 3 Game Day p. 53

■ Decodable Words

TARGET SKILLS: *Vowel Patterns: /ô/; Inflections*
all*, almost*, asked*, ball*, balls*, batting, cones, danced, dropped, faced, fall*, flopped, games, giggled, gliding, grabbed, grinning, hands*, hoops, hopping, kicked, knocked, kids, letting*, looked*, missing*, needs*, pals, patted, playing*, racing, running*, scored, small*, smiled, smiling, soaked, sports, started*, steps, swinging, times*, treetops, walked*, weaving, winning, yelled, zipped

PREVIOUSLY TAUGHT SKILLS

after*, and*, as*, at*, back*, bag, bat, be*, beam, beanbag, began*, best*, better*, between*, big*, but*, class, cool, crowd, day*, did*, didn't*, do*, don't*, down*, each* end*, face, fast*, fell*, fire*, first*, five, for*, fun*, game, get*, go*, goal, good*, got*, grass, had*, hard*, head*, her*, high*, his*, hit, hot*, I*, in*, instead, is*, it*, Jay, Jay's, join*, joy, just*, kept*, kick, like*, lost, me*, Megan, mind*, mine, mom, my*, next*, nice*, race, Rob, sat*, she*, shook, six, so*, spend, still*, such*, teacher*, team, that*, that's, them*, then*, this*, time*, to*, today*, told, too*, truck, up*, us*, way*, we*, well*, when*, will*, win, wish*, with*

■ High-Frequency Words
REVIEW
done, think, warm, went, without, woman, work, worked

PREVIOUSLY TAUGHT
a, about, because, could, every, have, laughed, over, pulled, said, some, the, through, two, was, water, were, who, you're

BOOK 4 My Big Bike Race p. 61

■ Decodable Words

TARGET SKILLS: *Vowel Patterns: /ô/; Inflections*
all*, beating, bikes, biking, brakes, braking, bumped, clapping, clocking, clumps, crammed, dipped, flying*, filled, fixed, glided, grabbed, gripped, hopping, hurts*, leading, lined*, logs, lots*, needs*, parts, perched, popped, racing, riding*, rocks*, roots, sides*, skidded, skidding, skipping, smiling, spinning, spitting, started*, steps, stopping*, tied*, tires, trails, turned*, weaved, wheels, woods, zigzagged

PREVIOUSLY TAUGHT SKILLS

and*, as*, back*, bag, be*, before*, best*, big*, bike, bottle, brake, came*, car*, chain, check, dad, day*, didn't*, dirt, do*, down*, drove, each*, ease, fall*, fast*, felt*, finish, first*, fix, flew, for*, gaze, go*, good*, had*, hard*, has*, head*, help*, hill, hit, huge, I*, if*, in*, into*, it*, its*, jump*, keep*, kept*, last, left*, like*, line*, long*, make*, me*, mom, my*, no*, off*, oil*, on*, onto, out*, past, patch, peak, pump, race, ramp, ride*, roof, safe, saw*, so*, sped, start*, steep, stuff, test, that*, that's*, then*, these*, thicker, thing*, this*, time*, to*, too*, took*, top, trail, tree*, turn*, up*, use*, way*, we*, week, when*, with*, you*, zip, zone

■ High-Frequency Words
REVIEW
there, went, without, work, working

PREVIOUSLY TAUGHT
a, also, anything, are, because, coming, could, every, funny, goes, never, of, one, over, pictures, should, sure, the, they, want, was, water, were

BOOK 1 Sports Played with a Ball p. 69

■ Decodable Words
TARGET SKILL: *Inflections*

batting, bigger, bounces, called*, flies*, kicked, misses*, pitcher, pitching, played*, playing*, rolled, running*, tosses, tried*, tries*, using*

PREVIOUSLY TAUGHT SKILLS

after*, all*, an*, and*, arms, as*, at*, back*, ball*, balls*, base, baseball, bases, bat, bats, bit, brain, brown*, but*, by*, can*, can't*, catch, chests, contests, do*, don't*, each* feet, few*, find*, first*, fit, football, for*, forth, fun*, game, games, get*, goal, goals, good*, grow*, hands*, has*, help*, helps*, hit, hits, home*, how*, if*, in*, inside*, into*, is*, it*, just*, keep*, keeps*, kick, kickball, legs, like*, line*, lines*, makes, may*, mitt, more*, most*, name*, need*, net, not*, odd, on*, or*, out*, outs*, pass*, past, person, places*, plate, play*, points*, post, races, racket, run*, runs*, same*, say*, score, scores, shake, shape, side*, skill, small*, soccer, softer, sport, sports, stands, start*, step, stop*, tag, takes*, team, team's, teams, tennis, test, that*, them*, these*, this*, time*, to*, too*, trade, try*, U.S.A., until*, use*, when*, wins, with*, you*

■ High-Frequency Words
REVIEW

move, thank, their, things, through

PREVIOUSLY TAUGHT

a, are, four, from, have, one, other, others, over, people, someone, the, they, three, two, what, work, your

BOOK 2 Sports Played in Water p. 77

■ Decodable Words
TARGET SKILL: *Inflections*

based, beaches, called*, copies, crashing, diving, facing, floating, heated, judges, jumping*, kicking, lined*, making*, played*, pointed*, races, racing, riding*, rowing, stories*, surfing, swimming, tries*

PREVIOUSLY TAUGHT SKILLS

all*, and*, arms, as*, at*, back*, beach, beat, before*, bend, big*, boats, breath, but*, butterfly, can*, catch, cold*, days*, deep, dive, dives, do*, each*, fast*, fastest, feet, few*, find*, first*, fit, flat, for*, fun*, get*, go*, group*, hands*, hard*, harder, head*, helps*, highest, hold*, hot*, how*, in*, into*, is*, it*, it's*, just*, keep*, kick, kind*, kinds*, legs, lie, like*, long*, looks*, lots*, master, may*, maybe*, meets, members, more*, most*, need*, not*, on*, or*, out*, paddle, part, person, pick, place*, places*, points*, pools, quite, race, ride*, row, rowboats, same*, score, scores, shell, shells, shore, simple, sit*, sits*, song's, speed, sport, sports, stand, summer, surf, swim, take*, takes*, team, tell*, tells*, than*, that*, them*, these*, this*, those*, time*, to*, toes, too*, train, turn*, twist, under*, up*, wave, waves, way*, when*, which*, while*, wins, winter, with*, you*

■ High-Frequency Words
REVIEW

eight, enough, goes, moves, their, through

PREVIOUSLY TAUGHT

a, another, are, doesn't, have, many, music, of, one, ones, people, some, the, they, together, water, what, who, would, year

BOOK 3 **Sports Played on Ice** p. 85

■ Decodable Words
TARGET SKILLS: *Inflections; Long* e (ie, y, ey)
called*, chief, curling, fancy, flying*, getting*, goalie, hockey, icy, key, padding, played*, skating, snowy, starting*, trying*

PREVIOUSLY TAUGHT SKILLS
after*, all*, an*, and*, at*, back*, big*, blades, bobsled, bobsleds, boots, bottom, brooms, brush, but*, by*, can*, center, close*, cold*, cross, do*, down*, each*, fast*, faster, fastest, fine, finish, first*, fit, flat, foot, for*, form, forth, freeze, fun*, get*, gets*, glide, go*, good*, hard*, has*, helmets, help*, high*, hills, hit, hot*, hurt*, ice, in*, inside*, into*, is*, it*, it's*, job, jump*, jumps, keep*, lakes, lap, large, left*, let*, like*, line*, long*, make*, marks, not*, on*, onto, or*, part, past, person, places*, play*, points*, ponds, puck, pucks, race, races, right*, rink, rinks, roses, rubber, scores, see*, sharp, shift, short, skate, skates, sleds, slide, slides, slow*, small*, smart, so*, speed, spin, sport, sports, stay*, steel, sticks, stone, stones, summers, sweep, take*, team, team's, teams, that*, them*, then*, these*, thick, this*, time*, times*, to*, too*, toss, toys, track, train, turns*, twirl, twists, up*, use*, way*, well*, when*, while*, win, wins, winter, with*

■ High-Frequency Words
REVIEW
enough, goes, move, moves, thank, their, things, through

PREVIOUSLY TAUGHT
a, another, are, around, four, from, front, music, of, other, others, people, some, sure, the, they, two, what, who

---

BOOK 4 **Track and Field** p. 93

■ Decodable Words
TARGET SKILLS: *Inflections; Long* e (ie, y, ey)
being*, dropped, field, holding*, jumping*, key, letting*, passes*, pointy, pumping, running*, thrilling, tossing* tricky, tries*

PREVIOUSLY TAUGHT SKILLS
all*, and*, as*, at*, bars, be*, bursts, but*, can*, contest, contests, cross, disks, do*, down*, each*, if*, end*, fall*, far*, fast*, feet, fence, finish, get*, good*, hands*, has*, he*, high*, highest, hit, how*, hurdle, hurdles, if*, in*, into*, is*, it*, it's*, judges, jump*, jumps*, kids, kinds*, knees, knock, lane, lanes, laps, leap, legs, like*, long*, longer, longest, make*, mark, may*, more*, most, must*, next*, nine, not*, off*, on*, onto, or*, out*, part, person, place*, plank, pole, quick, quite, race, races, rests, run*, runs*, runway, same*, see*, she*, short, skills, sky*, small*, speed, sports, start*, stick, take*, takes*, team, teams, ten, test, tests, that*, then*, these*, thin, this*, those*, to*, toes, toss, track, try*, turns*, until*, upright, use*, will*, win, wins, with*, without*, you*

■ High-Frequency Words
REVIEW
their, things, through

PREVIOUSLY TAUGHT
a, are, around, four, of, one, other, over, people, push, some, the, they, they're, three, very, watch, who

MODULE 12 ■ WEEK 1

BOOK 1 Why Rabbits Have Short Tails p. 101

■ Decodable Words

TARGET SKILL: *Suffixes -ful, -less, -ly, -y*

endless, fluffy, fuzzy, hardly, loudly, mighty, quickly, weakly

PREVIOUSLY TAUGHT SKILLS

all*, and*, as*, asked*, at*, back*, ball*, better*, big*, boasts, bragged, but*, came*, can*, catch, clip, cold*, come*, cut*, day*, did*, do*, doing*, don't*, dropped, fact, feel*, first*, fish*, fishing, for*, fox, fox's, freeze, freezing, frozen, gave*, gems, going*, had*, he*, help*, hide, him*, his*, hole, hook, I*, I'll*, I'm*, ice, in*, into*, is*, it*, its*, knew*, lake, left*, let*, lifted, like*, long*, look*, made*, make*, me*, mine, more*, my*, need*, night*, now*, on*, ouch, past, place*, plan*, proud, quite, rabbit, rabbits, saw*, see*, short, six, so*, sparkle, stay*, stuck, sunrise, tail, tails, talk*, ten, than*, that*, then*, this*, tied, time*, tired, to*, too*, trade, trick, tried*, tug, until*, waited*, went*, when*, why*, will*, wish*, with*, won't*, woods, yelped, you*

■ High-Frequency Words

REVIEW

again, says, what

PREVIOUSLY TAUGHT

a, answered, any, are, bear, could, every, four, have, here, of, one, pretty, push, put, said, the, there, was, water, would, your

BOOK 2 Why Possums Have Furless Tails p. 109

■ Decodable Words

TARGET SKILL: *Suffixes -ful, -less, -ly, -y*

boastful, furless, graceful, loudly, quickly, silky, slowly

PREVIOUSLY TAUGHT SKILLS

all*, also*, am*, and*, as*, at*, bald, be*, beat, began*, best*, better*, black*, brag, brush, brushed, but*, came*, can*, claws, day*, do*, don't*, down*, drumming, drums, face, fell*, felt*, fine*, for*, fox, fur, gave*, got*, ground*, had*, he*, head*, held*, help*, hid, high*, himself*, his*, holding*, holds*, I*, in*, insect, into*, is*, it*, its*, joy, last, lay, left*, like*, long*, look*, looks*, makes*, me*, meeting, mine, miss*, much*, must*, my*, need*, new*, nice, night*, not*, off*, old*, on*, pile, place*, please*, pointed*, porch, possum, possums, pride, puzzled, rabbit, ribbon, sang, sat*, saw*, scales, see*, send, sent, sharp, she*, side*, sitting*, sleep*, smile, smooth, snipping, so*, soon*, sound, space, starts*, stayed*, tail, tails, take*, thank*, that*, that's*, then*, thing*, this*, time*, to*, tonight, too*, took*, trim, until*, up*, wake, walked*, well*, went*, why*, will*, with*, you*

■ High-Frequency Words

REVIEW

above, around, does, gives, giving, says

PREVIOUSLY TAUGHT

a, about, animals, done, everyone, from, have, heard, laughed, of, said, someone, the, they're, was, where, your

BOOK 3 **Why Rabbits and Snakes Don't Mix** p. 117

■ Decodable Words
TARGET SKILLS: *Suffixes* -ful, -less, -ly, -y; *Prefixes* un-, re-
restated, returned, unwise

PREVIOUSLY TAUGHT SKILLS
all*, an*, and*, as*, asked*, at*, back*, bank, bet, big*, bite,
both*, brook, brown*, budge, called*, can*, can't*, contest, day*,
did*, do*, don't*, drink, each*, end*, find*, for*, gasped, gave*,
get*, giggled, going*, good*, got*, had*, happen*, hard*,
hardest, he*, him*, himself*, hissed, hopped, how*, I*, I'll*, I'm*,
if*, inch, into*, is*, joke, kept*, knew*, know*, leaned, left*,
let's*, long*, looks*, mad, made*, may*, might*, mix , must*,
next*, not*, now*, off*, on*, out*, play*, rabbit, rabbits, red*,
right*, rules, same*, sat*, saw*, see*, set*, sign, sit*, small*,
snake, snakes, snorted, snorting, so*, sound, start*, stay*, swam,
swim, take*, that*, that's*, them*, then*, this*, to*, told, tree*,
tricked, tug, tugged, tugging, under*, up*, us*, vine, we*, weak,
went*, when*, why*, will*, with*, won't*, wow, yell, yelled, you*

■ High-Frequency Words
REVIEW
again, give, live, lives, what

PREVIOUSLY TAUGHT
a, are, away, from, have,
of, often, one, other, said,
the, their, there, they,
very, was, watch, water,
who, would

BOOK 4 **Why Rabbits Run Fast** p. 125

■ Decodable Words
TARGET SKILLS: *Suffixes* -ful, -less, -ly, -y; *Prefixes* un-, re-
brainless, loudly, pointless, repeated, return, unkind, unwell

PREVIOUSLY TAUGHT SKILLS
all*, am*, and*, as*, asked*, at*, back*, be*, beat, beating,
began*, beside, best*, big*, boast, bragging, but*, came*, can*,
can't*, cheered, clapped, dad, dashed, day*, did*, down*, each*,
end*, fast*, faster, fastest, feel*, feet, find*, first*, flopped,
found*, ground*, had*, hard*, harder, hatched, he*, heap, help*,
her*, herself*, hi, hid, hill, hills, hilltop, his*, home*, hopped,
how*, huff, I*, I'll*, in*, into*, it*, it's*, just*, leaps, let's*, line*,
me*, meet, met, moaned, mom, nap, need*, needed*, next*, no*,
noon, now*, off*, out*, path, plan*, popped, puffing, rabbit,
rabbits, race, racing, ran*, reach*, reached*, rock*, run*, sang,
saw*, second, see*, she*, side*, slowpoke, so*, starting, stayed*,
stop*, stumped, take*, than*, that*, that's*, then*, these*, think*,
this*, time*, to*, top, town, trick, true, turtle, turtle's, up*, use*,
we*, well*, when*, why*, will*, win*, woke, woods, yes*, you*,
zipping, zoomed

■ High-Frequency Words
REVIEW
above, again, around

PREVIOUSLY TAUGHT
a, about, animals, from,
have, here, laughed,
laughing, never, of, other,
over, pretty, said, the, they,
together, two, was, your

MODULE 12 ■ WEEK 2

= High-Frequency Word

BOOK 1 Music Under the Sea p. 133

■ Decodable Words

TARGET SKILL: *Two-Syllable Words: CV, CVC*

also*, baby*, bedtime, clover, concerts, cozy, delay, even*, music*, open*, over*, picnics, relax, replay, replied, tonight, tulip, under*, unkind, until*

PREVIOUSLY TAUGHT SKILLS

all*, and*, ask*, at*, back*, band, be*, beat, best*, bit, brightly, but*, called*, came*, can*, crab, crabs, cried*, dad, day*, don't*, down*, feet, fine, flute, glad, good*, harp, he*, her*, hi*, his*, hold*, home*, hope, horn, I*, in*, instead, is*, it*, jazz, jazzy, just*, kept*, knocked, like*, likes*, loud, louder, loudly, low, make*, marched, mean, mom, morning, name*, named*, need*, next*, night*, not*, now*, on*, out*, parks, play*, played*, playing*, plays*, please*, right*, scales, sea*, see*, she*, sing*, sings*, sleep*, slow*, slowly, smiled, smooth, so*, songs, sounds, star, stars, stop*, stopped*, sway, sweet, sweetly, swung, tap, taps, tell*, that*, that's*, them*, to*, tone, too*, voice*, we*, we'll*, we're*, well*, will*, with* you*

■ High-Frequency Words
REVIEW

once, these, they, water, who

PREVIOUSLY TAUGHT

a, again, animals, come, could, door, family, family's, have, hear, lives, of, one, said, sure, the, their, together, very, would

BOOK 2 We Need Water p. 141

■ Decodable Words

TARGET SKILL: *Two-Syllable Words: CV, CVC*

also*, birdbaths, bottles, buckets, droplets, frozen, garden, humans, little*, protect, puddles, rivers*

PREVIOUSLY TAUGHT SKILLS

add, all*, and*, as*, at*, back*, baths, be*, beaches, big*, birds*, blue*, bring*, brush, can*, catch, clean*, clouds, cold*, cooking, cows, creeks, cubes, do*, down*, drain, drink, drinks, drop, drops, dry, fall*, falls*, find*, flows, for*, form, forms, fresh, gas, get*, globe, go*, gold, good*, ground*, grow*, hail, hands*, has*, help*, hike, home*, homes*, how*, huge, ice, if*, in*, into*, is*, it*, join*, just*, keep*, keeping*, lakes, land*, lands*, last, let*, like*, long*, look*, looks*, lug, make*, might*, miles, more*, much*, must*, need*, not*, on*, or*, pails, pick*, pipes, plants*, ponds, pumps, rain*, rise, roots, run*, runs*, sea*, see*, shape, sheep, shows*, sky*, sleet, small*, snow, stay*, take*, takes*, taking*, teeth, than*, that*, them*, then*, things*, time*, to*, too*, trash, try*, tubs, up*, us*, use*, used*, waste, we*, wells, when*, wild, will*, wisely, with*, you*

■ High-Frequency Words
REVIEW

people, these, they, wash, water, who, world

PREVIOUSLY TAUGHT

a, again, animals, around, become, comes, different, every, from, have, live, living, of, one, our, some, the, their, what, your

BOOK 3 Jobs That Use Water p. 149

■ Decodable Words

TARGET SKILL: *Two-Syllable Words: CV, CVC*

after*, artists, cannot*, dentists, markets, paper, pilots, sunny, super, under*, without*

PREVIOUSLY TAUGHT SKILLS

added, all*, and*, armed, art, at*, back*, be*, big*, blue*, boat, boats, bring*, can*, can't*, car*, cars*, catch, check, clay, clean*, cooking, corn, cows, crops, cross, cups, cuts, dads, day*, did*, dishes, dive, do*, drink, dry, eating*, far*, farm, farmers, farming, farms, fish*, fishing, fly*, foods*, for*, forces, fun*, germs, get*, glue, go*, goats, grow*, help*, hens, hoses, hot*, how*, if*, in*, into*, is*, it*, it's*, jets, job, jobs, jump*, keep*, kids, kinds*, lakes, land*, letting*, lines*, long*, look*, lots*, make*, may*, might*, milk, mix, moms, must*, need*, needed*, nets, new*, nurses, off*, on*, or*, out*, over*, paint, paints, pans, peaches, plums, pools, pots, reach*, rid, right*, safe, sail, sea*, shape, sheep, ship, ships, short, soap, soapy, stay*, still*, swim, swimming, take*, teach, teeth, that*, them*, things*, to*, too*, trips, us*, use*, uses*, vases, waves, we*, well*, wheat, when*, with*, you*

■ High-Frequency Words

REVIEW

people, people's, these, they, wash, washing, water, who, world

PREVIOUSLY TAUGHT

a, animals, another, are, buy, colors, ever, many, of, other, our, some, the, their, watch, work

---

BOOK 4 Car Wash p. 157

■ Decodable Words

TARGET SKILL: *Two-Syllable Words: CV, CVC*

after*, bathtub, dirty, follow*, inside*, open*, rivers*, windows*

PREVIOUSLY TAUGHT SKILLS

all*, also*, and*, at*, big*, bright, buses, but*, by*, called*, can*, can't*, car*, cars*, clean*, cleaning*, cloths, coins, dad, dad's, did*, dirt, do*, doing*, down*, drains, drive, drop, dry, dust, fit, flows, for,* get*, go*, good*, grass, grime, ground*, hand*, has*, helps*, home*, hose, hoses, how*, huge, I*, in*, into*, is*, it*, jets, job, keep*, kind*, lakes, last, look*, means, more*, mud, must*, my*, need*, next*, nice, off*, on*, or*, out*, pails, past, pay, place*, places*, rags, rides*, right*, rigs, rub, see*, self, shine, shoot, shoots, shut, slots, so*, soak, soap, soapy, soft, space, spaces, spot, stay*, steps, still*, swirl, swirls, swoop, take*, tanks, that*, that's*, them*, then*, this*, to*, too*, track, trucks, use*, using*, vans, we*, wet, will*, with*, yard, you*

■ High-Frequency Words

REVIEW

people, these, they, wash, washes, washing, water, who

PREVIOUSLY TAUGHT

a, about, another, comes, goes, have, moves, of, ones, our, the, what

BOOK 1 Claws Swipe p. 165

■ Decodable Words
TARGET SKILL: *Suffixes -er, -est*
faster, fastest, slowest

PREVIOUSLY TAUGHT SKILLS
all*, also*, an*, and*, ant, ants, as*, at*, back*, bark, be*, beetles, black, branches, bugs, but*, can*, cat, cat's, cats, claws, clean*, cling, close*, cool, dark, defend, depend, dig, digging, digs, do*, dog, down*, eat*, eats*, find*, fingers, flat, food*, for*, fur, get*, gets*, grab, groom, grooming, grow*, grubs, handy, hang, hangs, has*, help*, hold*, home*, hooks, house*, hunt, hurt*, if*, in*, insects, inside*, instead, into*, is*, it*, itch, its*, itself*, kinds*, leaves*, like*, logs, long*, look*, makes*, mark, may*, mice, mole, moles, moss, nails, needs*, nest, nests, not*, off*, on*, or*, out*, owl, pads, pal's, paw, pops, quite, rabbits, really*, rips, roots, see*, shaped, sharp, short, sloth's, slow*, slowly, small*, snakes, so*, soil, space, stay*, stuck, stuff, swipe, take*, than*, that*, them*, things*, thinks*, this*, those*, time*, tips, to*, toes, too*, tree*, trees*, tunnels, underground, up*, upside, use*, useful, uses*, way*, well*, when*, will*, with*, you*, yucky, yummy

■ High-Frequency Words
REVIEW

animal, animals, could, different, won't

PREVIOUSLY TAUGHT

a, almost, are, bear, bears, come, from, have, many, moves, of, one, other, people, some, the, their, they, where, world

BOOK 2 Teeth Chomp p. 173

■ Decodable Words
TARGET SKILL: *Suffixes -er, -est*
longest, lower, sharper, sharpest, smaller

PREVIOUSLY TAUGHT SKILLS
all*, always*, and*, as*, at*, back*, be*, beaver, before*, behind, big*, bites, bits, bones, bumpy, but*, called*, can*, catch, chewing, chomp, chop, cow, crush, cut*, dam, dams, dead, did*, dig, digs, down*, dull, eat*, eating*, eats*, even*, fangs, feet, finds*, fish*, flat, food*, for*, forests, frogs, gator, get*, glad, grab, grass, grasslands, grind, grow*, growing*, gulp, had*, has*, help*, helpful, hold*, how*, if*, in*, insects, instead, into*, it*, its*, kinds*, know*, large*, like*, long*, look*, lots*, make*, makes*, males, meat, most*, much*, new*, nipping, no*, not*, old*, on*, pad, parts*, pieces, plains, plant*, plants*, pond, press, prize, reach*, replace, rivers*, roots, shakes, shapes, sharp, sizes, slice, small*, smile, so*, spaces, stay*, stones, stop*, teeth, that*, them*, thick, this*, those*, time*, to*, too*, top, trees*, tusks, up*, use*, uses*, which*, wide, win, with*, wood, yes*, you*

■ High-Frequency Words
REVIEW

animal, animals, could, different, pulling, pulls, should, would

PREVIOUSLY TAUGHT

a, are, carries, come, does, enough, from, front, have, live, lives, many, never, of, one, ones, other, push, some, the, their, wants, water, what, where

BOOK 3 **Horns Help** p. 181

■ Decodable Words
TARGET SKILLS: *Suffixes* -er, -est; *Inflections*
billies, biting, digging, getting, jabbed, named*, shaggy, shorter, thicker, warmer

PREVIOUSLY TAUGHT SKILLS
an*, and*, antlers, as*, at*, baby*, bark, bash, battle, beasts, big*, bighorn, bighorns, billy, bit, black*, bone, buds, bumps, but*, cactuses, called*, can*, catch, cats, cow, curled, defending, do*, don't*, eat*, elk, elk's, fangs, female, fingers, for*, fuzz, gets*, go*, goat, goats, grow*, habit, has*, he*, head*, heads*, help*, high*, hills, his*, horn, horns, hunt, hunting, I*, if*, in*, insects, into*, is*, it*, its*, itself*, jab, keep*, kid, kids, let*, like*, made*, make*, male, may*, me*, meat, nails, new*, no*, nose, not*, off*, on*, or*, out*, pester, pine, plants*, playing*, poke, protect, ram, rams, rub, same*, say*, sharp, shed, sheep, smell, soft, sort, spikes, spines, stuff, than*, that*, that's*, them*, then*, these*, things*, this*, those*, times*, to*, toes, top, trees*, try*, unlike, up*, use*, uses*, velvet, when*, who*, will*, with*, without*, you*

■ High-Frequency Words
REVIEW
animal, animals, could, different talk, won't, would

PREVIOUSLY TAUGHT
a, are, away, from, gives, have, live, of, ones, only, other, some, the, their, your

BOOK 4 **Spines Jab** p. 189

■ Decodable Words
TARGET SKILLS: *Suffixes* -er, -est; *Inflections*
dropped, jabbed, poked, poking, rattling, shaking, swimming

PREVIOUSLY TAUGHT SKILLS
also*, an*, and*, at*, back*, ball*, be*, belly, between*, big*, birds*, bite, blend, boo, by*, called*, can*, can't*, close*, crabs, cracks, dirt, eat*, feet*, few*, find*, fish*, flat, for*, fright, get*, gets*, glad, go*, gobble, grab, hard*, has*, head*, hedgehog, help*, helps*, hide, hold*, horns, how*, hunt, I*, if*, in*, into*, is*, it*, its*, itself, jab, jam, keep*, know*, lashes, leaves*, less, lie, like*, likely, long*, look*, makes*, may*, might*, on*, otters, ouch, out*, picks*, place*, points*, pointy, pop, prickles, prickly, puffing, puffs, quickly, quills, reptile, reptile's, rocks*, roll, run*, safe*, sand, say*, sea*, sharp, skin, snack, so*, spikes, spines, starts, stick, sticking, such*, tail, that*, them*, then*, these*, this*, thorn, time*, to*, too*, try*, tucks, turtles, up*, urchins, useful, when*, with*, yet, you*

■ High-Frequency Words
REVIEW
animal, animal's, animals, could, pull, should, talk, won't, would

PREVIOUSLY TAUGHT
a, again, are, been, colors, comes, coming, ever, from, gives, have, having, lives, many, other, something, sure, the, their, very, want, what, where